Contact with the Wild
Prose Poems

Contact with the Wild

Prose Poems

Kim Chinquee

MadHat Press
Cheshire, Massachusetts

MadHat Press
MadHat Incorporated
PO Box 422, Cheshire, MA 01225

Copyright © 2025 Kim Chinquee
All rights reserved.

The Library of Congress has assigned
this edition a Control Number of
2025933961

ISBN 978-1-952335-96-9 (paperback)

Words by Kim Chinquee
Cover design by Joan Wilking

www.MadHat-Press.com

First Printing
Printed in the United States of America

to the animals

Table of Contents

Libraries Of Time	1
Day One, or Maybe Two	2
The Pilot	3
Full and Bloated	4
Time Is a Circle	5
A Whole Team	6
Drop the Mic	7
A Thousand Pages	8
You've Reached Your Destination	10
A Big Square	11
Clumped in a Huddle	13
The Circus Is in Town	14
Contact With the Wild	15
Swimming Underwater	17
The Soft Parts	18
The Upper Parts	19
Rattles	20
Athlete	21
Spinner	22
Clean	23
Birdwatcher	24
The Car	25
Funhouse	26
A Tiny Army	27
Pipette	29
Breaking Bread	30
Botanical	32
Stay Awake	33
The Closest Thing	34
My Inheritance	35
All Over the Planets	36

Contents

Dramatic	37
Delightful	38
High and Wide	40
Billiards	41
On One Side	42
Her Way	43
Rare	44
About the Hour	45
Spoonful	46
Please, Just Come to the Door	47
Existence	49
Life-Sized	50
Independence	51
Smiley	56
High as Streetlights	58
Sleepwalker	59
Go to the Clouds	60
Confetti	61
The Man	62
Around the World	63
Underwater	65
Into the Nose	66
Snout	67
Studies of the Senses	68
Sketches of Her	75
Cellar	76
Machinery	78
Marathoner	79
Runaways	80
Jumper	81
Candy-Striper	83
Hybrid	84
Climbers	85
Theoretician	86

Perennial	87
Floating on an Ocean	88
Red Zero	89
A Borrowed Canoe	90
Plumbing	91
Neverland	92
Speed Dial	93
Acknowledgments	95
About the Author	97

Libraries Of Time

I cook listening to the book, drive listening to the book, sit in waiting rooms reading the book, fall asleep reading the book. Unlike a protagonist in the book, I don't go to bed starving. Like the protagonist in the book, I don't have a sweetie pie, don't hear a drumroll. The book is over six-hundred pages. Covers libraries of time. Parts of the book reenact parts of other parts of another book within the book, and has children wearing costumes, reenacting yet other parts of the book. I wait at the doctor's office with the book, then later, after a phlebotomist hurries to take my blood, telling me to make a fist, her finger palpating my vein, I drive home listening to the book, my wheels turning, my mind living in the world of the book. Wheels in the book are described as stratospheres, donuts, things that whirl. I turn the pages like wheels make things move, like the wheels on my bikes, the wheels of my mind, my memories, my words, wheels like vehicles through time. Books like wheels, and wheels like books, moving past worlds, universes, galaxies, centuries beyond me.

Day One, or Maybe Two

There are people stuck in cars. There's a driving ban, save essential workers. The essential workers are getting stuck and the rescue teams trying to rescue the essential workers are getting stuck, snowplows are getting stuck trying to rescue the rescue teams, and finally the city gives up. Three people have already been confirmed dead and there are probably already more people dead in cars. It'll take a while to find the abandoned cars, the abandoned bodies, the abandoned pets and children. Some folks call for help on a social media website. Loved ones have lost phone charge. Power, gas. There are babies needing respirators. Mothers giving birth. Diabetics. People needing oxygen. Water, food. We're urged to stay inside. I have heat. I have power. I have internet, a computer. My TV. I have a fireplace. I have food and shelter. It's Christmas Eve, 2022. I hear the constant howl of the wind, see the madness of the tree limbs. My windows shake. Meteorologists call this a cat-three hurricane with snow, the biggest weather event in Western New York's history. Every hour or so, I don boots, a hat, a coat and gloves, and I shovel a path to my furnace vent, to clear it, to make sure my dogs and I don't die of carbon monoxide poisoning. Two people, a mother and son, have already died from that.

The Pilot

In the middle of a blizzard, my dreams welcome me to skies. I'm my own pilot, on a motorcycle, flying over trees like ponderosa pines, kokerbooms, then I become a Humvee with a checkbook, overseeing a factory full of plums. On the ground, I develop a niche for creating the most exotic fruitcakes.

Full and Bloated

Hearing the roar of the thunder, the windows brightening and shaking, I cook, listening to yet another audiobook: a novel about a farm town like the one where I grew up. I hear of corn fields, cows, and it brings me back there. The smell of the manure, the cold nose of a calf as I feed her the mixed formula I felt with my own hands: a night chore every evening, as my sister took the mornings. I don't eat meat now, cooking vegetables, tofu that I've learned works best if I press it before freezing, then again after it thaws. It absorbs the seasoning. Curry. That's what I smell now, and from the audiobook, the speaker talks of a dairy farm that burned, and I wonder about the animals. They're never mentioned. The book won awards. I wonder what might've happened if my family's farm burned down. It was in the family for centuries. Nothing burned, but my father got sick. He was the one to run the farm, didn't want to hire helpers. We had over a hundred acres, over a hundred milking cows. My sister and I had to milk them after he was hospitalized, after screaming out in church. I was thirteen. In the barn, there was a little stair that went into the parlor where we milked, and there's no way I'll ever forget that feeling: my dad in the hospital, my mom staying there with him, my sister and I and a neighbor boy who I was shy about just trying to keep up the farm. Cows came into the stalls. I cleaned their udders with a hose. They felt so full and bloated. I put on the milkers. My dad had shown me a few times how to milk, as if he knew there was something happening to him, as if he knew his daughters would have to take it on someday. It was obvious when the udders were empty, and when they were, we simply released each cow and opened the stall for the next one.

Time Is a Circle

Time is a circle in my dreams. I wake, thinking I'm a monk, but then I'm just me with earplugs and an eye mask, dressed in my warm robe, surrounded by blankets. It takes a while for me to realize there are no longer ramparts, no cobblestone roads, no wigs made of horsehair. I don't know how far I go back in my dreams, but it seems another century. I may have been reading too many books. In my dreams, all the people have halos. Like the characters in the book. I drift to sleep again, and take on a lighter sense of the book, its floating images, its haloed characters. My three dogs, also haloed, wake me again and beg to go out. I step down the stairs, lighthearted and light-footed, as if I were an angel myself, and I let them out into the backyard. I see halos on trees. Halos on the back garage. Halos all over everything. It's beautiful. It's nothing I've ever seen.

A Whole Team

I wake to blurry faces. You did good, says one. Another face connected to something else touches me. I try to think of where I am. Dreaming of a hockey stick, a lung. I say to the face, I've been dreaming about hockey. Dogs. All three of mine sitting around a table, eating nachos, drinking tea. I say, I have to pee. You have a catheter, says maybe a long face. I try to sit. My head's a brick. There's a whole team around me. They say, You need to stay down. There are tubes and machines. I hear hissing noises. Parts of me feel numb, though certain parts of me are so full of excitement.

Drop the Mic

I breakdance in my kitchen, cooking lentils, thinking of my piano days, my fingers on the keyboard. It could have been the perfect crime for me to win first place at my recital. It isn't in my genes, I guess, my mom suspecting I'd always be a failure. After she left my dad, he cried in church. They got therapy. I was left like a forearm, stuck eating a whole turkey. Vomiting. That's still in stereo-mode at times, but you learn to drop the mic. It's a shoehorn. It's a star flake. It's an amaryllis if it almost buds by Christmas. I go to the park. I have three dogs. I'm vegan now. As a child, my best friend was my cow. Her name was Iona.

A Thousand Pages

I fly. Not high, but low to the ground just to save myself from drowning. My best dreams involve color: water so clean I can see down to the coral, the swirling fish, creatures more kaleidoscopic than even in the movies. Beyond are mountains, moss, a sky so high. Spotty clouds arranged better than art. My last dream involves a boat, with holly trees. No birds, but full of dogs, including all those of my life. We're in the boat together. They play, and the boat keeps tipping, and the water's so deep and the sky is so high, but they don't care. They love me.

    I wake to thundersnow, opening the blinds. Snow so high it makes my life feel like a silhouette, a buried page, or maybe one especially folded in one of a thousand books of a thousand pages. I prepared for this. Yesterday, I went to Aldi's. I bought so much stuff I had to reorganize my pantry. I bought firewood, dog food, a new shovel. Fake salt—safe for the dogs—to melt ice from the sidewalk. I cooked, listening to music: Eva Cassidy, Nora Jones, all the things that soothe me. I took two walks, one with my friend, who thought he had a stroke. He's a week out of the hospital. His hand is still numb. I remembered I had that too once, about ten years ago, waking up to a hand I didn't recognize. It took nine months to get full feel back. He's a runner. A cyclist. Like me. I then went to the dog park, where my puppy and other dogs ran around, and my other friends showed up and we talked about how everything is closing but here there is no snow yet. Eight years ago was SnowVember. I remember because it's when a friend died. He was a race director. For the marathon. The Turkey Trot. He died of AFib. It was a surprise to us all. The Southtowns had eight feet of snow. Where I lived in North Buffalo only had a couple inches. I hear more thunder. It growls. I check my body parts. I try to shake another dream. The snow falls. My world says it isn't done yet.

You've Reached Your Destination

We're on trains and buses, testifying against criminals, then on a late-night plane to somewhere else. Something in my gut doesn't sit right, and I have a pain beneath my kneecap. I realize, as I write, this is no help to my reader. How can one escape a world that exists beyond the limits of one's body? What happens after you must sleep and fall into another land? It's not all dandelions and sunshine, says one ghost to me. I'm not a ghost, I say. And then one laughs and says maybe I am.

A Big Square

Behind one thin eyelid, I see inside a dollar. The dollar is flat, and looking at its tiny spine, I see its world opening: a room, a printing press in the 1800s, a stereotype, upper cases, lower cases, people out of sorts. The dollar turns into a book with a thick spine, and from the outside, if you manipulate its fore-edge, there's a picture of a princess holding a domino in one hand, and in the other, a melting cube. But I fly deeper through the fore-edge, where I watch a hunched bald man in spectacles hold his linotype, picking letters with his fingers from his cases as he makes the typeset for the book of which I'm in. Welcome, he says. Sit. He doesn't say anything about my running shoes, my shorts and sweaty hair. He says, You look exhausted. He goes back to his intentions. He wears a vest under his suit coat. The air smells of mold, cigars and whiskey. Then he turns into my grandpa in his work clothes, and next to him is my grandma at the kitchen with her spoon, preparing stuffing. Well, hello there, child, she says. I morph into the child I once was, in jeans with patches on the knees, a halter top, my skin full of scabs from the time I fell off the ladder to the hayloft. My grandma says, You were always careless. My dad appears like he always did on the farm where I grew up, out of nowhere, kicking cows, and dogs and cats. One cat, while trying to give birth, gave up and walked around for days with her unborn kittens still hanging from inside her. My dad kicked the cat and said, Stupid cat. She died not long after. I saw her body where my dad discarded the animals after they were dead, and we didn't intend to eat them. She was a calico cat that I'd named Calico. I'd tamed her as a kitten. After that, she was always rubbing up against me when I'd go out to feed the calves, when I'd go out for some company, when I wanted someone just to talk to.

We had a lot of cats. We had a lot of dogs. We had cows and calves and heifers and goats and kids, and I loved that they were always there. They were more than just animals. I'm deep in the book, traveling through its pages, to the creek I used to visit as a girl, putting my feet in the water, feeling the current, the cold stone, watching the minnows so busy without probably having to think. I look up and watch the clouds move, and as I hear a dog bark, I hit my head against the book's edges and its boundaries, spine. As I spill out of the book, I see my dog in front of me, her wide sweet face, smiling and panting. I feel my legs and arms. My neck. See the contents of my room. My dog presents to me her paw, simply asking to be let out again.

Clumped in a Huddle

In the basement, I find a Catwoman costume, a stuffed chickadee, a portrait of my relatives clumped in a huddle. I don't recognize the people in the still, though think one guy is my late grandpa as a teen, and maybe his late brother, when they used to play ball in the yard. There's a pair of my son's baby shoes, which I hope to give to him one day. I remember the Catwoman costume from the year a colleague had a party—and somewhere still on Facebook there's a picture: me, as Catwoman and a Batman, a Spiderman and a life-sized empanada. It was when we all got along, before I went up for promotion, before a colleague died, before another got divorced and one left for another institution. I'm not sure why these random things are in a box together. I imagine I packed hastily during my last move, and some boxes aren't unpacked yet. Every other year, my whole street has a sale. It's been going on over a couple dozen years, and this one is my second. Last time, people were still kind of COVID-scared. This time, I want to take part. Also, though I have a ton of storage, I have too much stuff, some unused in ages: CDs, DVDs, a couple vacuum cleaners, paintings, clothes, lamps, bike accessories, kitchen appliances and dishes. I find an album of pictures I took of my son as a baby. I hug it, bring it upstairs, and look through memories of when he started walking, lost a tooth, gatherings of his several birthday parties. There's a picture of our dog, Menthol, who howled every time we cut an onion, which earned him the nickname Baby. I take pictures of the pictures, and text them to my daughter-in-law, who just moved their stuff and pets to their new home. My son is army infantry, a soldier. He's just been deployed, serving in a war zone.

The Circus Is in Town

Let's skip a day, I say to my dog, of going to the park. We live in a college town, full of left- handed scholars, shapeshifters, administrative thugs. I cook collard greens, adding every kind of spice. My dog looks up at me, jumps, resting her paws, her jaw, onto the surface of me.

Contact With the Wild

I tilt my head as I brush my teeth, making sure to get to the back and corners: my crowns and molars, gums. From my phone, Mary Oliver's voice recites a poem about a grasshopper, how it rests on her hand. I imagine it blinking. I imagine them making eye contact, if a grasshopper can do that. In my Nature Writing class, I have students read Annie Dillard's piece "Living Like Weasels," and I imagine eye contact with the wild, the eye contact I had with the cows on the farm where I grew up. I remember eating parts of those same cows, after helping my parents pack up their meat and stack them in the freezer. I have eye contact with my dogs—they look at me with their heads tilted, as if trying to understand me. They probably know me better than any living thing—they see me night and day, and at times I wonder how I look in their eyes; they're forgiving, patient, though not so patient when it comes to wanting treats and food and asking to be let out of the yard and then back in, especially in the morning. Mornings, my dreams braid into themselves; and this morning, after letting the dogs out, I fall back into a slumber, having a dream of a dream; in the dream I am in England with my sister and mom, and we compliment a handsome man in a suit and he says his name is Chris. He's dark-haired, tall, with a pronounced nose. Friendly, but occupied, and after saying goodbye, he gets on a chariot to accompany the Queen. Queen Elizabeth, who (like Oliver) is dead now, and I try to nudge my mom, try to say: Mom, he's with the Queen, but I can't speak. I keep trying to speak, but my body is stuck with the words that won't come out. When I wake (still in a dream), I realize that was a dream, and I tell my mom I dreamt I was trying to speak, that we met the man who accompanied the Queen, and she says she could see I was trying to speak in my dream. I'm relieved, waking from that dream, knowing I was dreaming; it feels merely like a speed bump. My mom gives me a necklace made of yarn, and someone sings a ballad. That blends with the sound of my dogs pawing at the door, a crunch crunch crunch sound, which wakes me up from the dream, and the dream I had of a dream. I feel my hands, my feet, my toes and look to the door, where my dogs are waiting, so I lift my body and go to the door and open it, letting them back into the house again.

Swimming Underwater

My spirit flies around, my finger touching the Big Dipper, my gut going underground, riding on the subway, which takes me to the sea, where I let an octopus wrap its arms around me. I become a fish, swimming underwater, and when I rise again, my wings take me to a pine tree, where leaves crunch underneath, and smells like smoke take me to my grandma: laughing her same laugh, her bad knees making her walk crooked. She floats, points, putting lights around the tree, and as she ascends, she tops it with an angel.

The Soft Parts

Summertime plays nearby, but Winter won't allow it. Winter blows its way through crowds of parents, infants, teens, the elderly, who thought they had a grasp on the worst storm in world history. Winter is an asshole, says Summertime and Spring. They have gifts, as proof. Just hear the birds sing! The tastes of fresh tomatoes, seeing melons ripen. Can you see the colors open in the fields, the yards, the porches? The sounds of children's footsteps, the voices of them laughing!? Autumn has no words, busy making every ground available for fallen leaves, plants requiring rest. Autumn provides for all the soft parts. Autumn welcomes Winter, not out of haste, nor out of spite for other Seasons. Autumn needs her slumber. When the snow falls, the seasons take big sighs and let Winter have its time.

The Upper Parts

It's not fair, she says to a random god above, to have to choose a Hangman phrase. With all the phones and other stuff, who even plays Hangman anymore? Oh, they do, says a rag from the corner. Hello! says a small voice from the upper parts of a solarium that no one will probably see during this day in 2023. Lots of things happen all over the place. She's not sure where she is now. She's stuck in a windmill. She's a golden retriever. She might as well be a bug, a gladiator. But you know where this girl is? She's small and lovely. She's escaping lots of trauma she doesn't even see as trauma until she must grow into an adult. She's putting her feet in the water again, feeling the stream against her feet. She feels the cold sensation. She's watching the minnows doing their things. She'll envision this throughout her life. She'll return to the same minnows, and they'll welcome her. They'll even jump out of the water if they must, telling her how excited they are to have her back again.

Rattles

When I finally woke up, the nurse handed me my baby. He's pretty, she said, plopping him. His eyes looked small. The sun shone in. I squinted. I tried to remember the last thing I remembered. A dance in the OR, people scrambling all around me. A nurse with horns. A doctor with a scalpel, another looking toothless. Their faces, all veiny. My husband, where was he, with a cherry. My baby cried, his voice squeaky. I hurt from where they took him. Shh, I said. Shh. I held him. I was cold. He got quiet, closed his eyes and I asked the nurse where was my husband. She wore scrubs with an array of colored rattles. Yellow glasses. Something smelled like apples. She said, Your baby's probably hungry. I tried to move my arms, to give him, but a sharp pain shot through me. Ahh! I said. Please, I said to the nurse. Can you? She took him, shushing him, bouncing him out to the hallway.

Athlete

My mom, my son, and I go to dinner at a place called Margarita's. My son has just flown in, his first visit here from college. I've just flown in too, from home in New York. We sit under the umbrella, making talk, eating chips and salsa. My son jumps over the rail, going to smoke in the lot. Two ladies say he must be an athlete. My mom sips her cocktail and says maybe later we can take a drive to see her brother's campsite. It'll take an hour to get there. I ask her what we'll do. My uncle is pleasant. I tell my mom I'm not sure. I remember my son and me when he was little. It was just us two. We'd rent these silly movies. We'd drive to find a sunset. We'd color with our noses. We'd make a pie and put it on a doorstep. We'd turn up the tape and dance. By the time the food comes, my son's back from his smoke and my mom's on her third happy hour special. I get a salad, skipping the sour cream, the shell. My mom gets a steak meal. My son opts for a fajita. It starts to rain, and then my mom says the campsite's out of the question. Finally, we all run to the car, saying the last one there is a raincoat.

Spinner

Let's elope for a day, I say to my ex-husband. But we already tried that, he says more than once. We weren't smart about money, ignoring the possibility of hedge funds, bonds, savings for our children.

We're still, like dust, clinging to the web of a spider.

Clean

As children, my mom and her siblings weren't allowed to bathe on a regular basis. They lived on a farm. My mom, on a regular basis, would remind me, when I was a child: her classmates would make fun of her, calling her dirty. She never seemed dirty to me, always making sure to clean the house, clean behind my ears, clean me of so much dirt that she would scrub me. We lived on a farm ourselves, and there's lots of dirt involved. She sang songs to me when she cleaned me, always cheerful in her singsong. My dad wasn't a singsong person. My dad was schizophrenic. His parents claimed to be clean in their church ways, going to services on Sundays. Preaching about the great news of the Lord. My grandfather looked clean on the surface, but he was dirty in his own ways. I clean myself on a regular basis. I clean my house on a regular basis. I have three dogs. They can make messes in the house. Growing up, our dogs weren't allowed in the house. They ran away on a regular basis.

Birdwatcher

At a nature writing workshop, I confessed I didn't like birds. They can prey onto a head. Their beaks are pointy, and they make weird noises. They seem so unclean. It's nice to see them in the sky with wings. I like to fly. I like to get on airplanes. Sometimes, when I run, I put my arms out.

Birds can peck at things, like my grandfather pecked away at my feelings and my innocence when I was small, and even in my teen years. He was a birdwatcher. He had all kinds of bird books and lived in the woods with his wife, my grandma, who was mouse-like, following him with her arms and hands and legs in her downright posture.

I live within my cells. The hypnotherapist I work with takes me deep while I nest into my room. We first catch up on Zoom, and then, on the phone, after moving to my bedroom, with my eyes closed, she's able to transport me. She helps me find my angel, with enormous wings, who takes me to fine places. I float on a cloud. Sometimes I resort to the creek on the farm where I grew up, where I used to visit frogs. I go low then high, where I find my spirits. She tells me they are me. I find my aunt, my uncle, dad, my grandpa, my one former therapist who jumped from a high-rise.

The Car

A Chevy Berlinetta. Her husband had surprised her. The sun began to set, and he drove them with the top down. She said to him she loved him. She didn't care about the car much. She drove it, pushing on the pedal. They went to the Gulf, which would be a hurricane much later, things destroyed and gone and folks: their future former neighbors with their shark boat, who they would grow attached to. She pressed her shoe to the pedal. It was a car much faster than either of them had beforehand.

Funhouse

I listen to the thunder, watch the snowdrops blooming in the yard, popping up with the winter's graduation. The whole yard's full of its white dots, a strange contrast to the snow that's finally melted, save a couple patches that stick around like stragglers. I shake off an itch to drive onto the freeway, finding some other new horizon, ones like I see on the TV, a geographical fix that will likely disappear as quick as the melting of chocolate in my mouth before having to swallow. I'm not even crazy about chocolate. I have nowhere to be. No one, from anywhere, is calling. Nothing's pressing except the hunger of my dogs, their barks, their need for water, food, belly rubs, my love. Rain falls, and I look up to the sky, wondering of science, the mixture in the atmosphere that turns its tricks like magic.

A Tiny Army

Taking inventory in my yard each spring serves as my elixir. Today the bearded iris opens, its purple petals out like wings, some of them curled, revealing bits of yellow, stripes of white. The stem of it is tall, announcing its presence amid ferns, columbines that surround and spread throughout the yard in their pastels, and nearby an oriental poppy sits yet in a bubble. I imagine it opening in fast forward, and if accompanied by an anthem, what would that anthem be? What's the most beautiful word? How could I, in all this enchantment, have any way to capture and describe it? I find more columbines: angle my camera lens to capture the magic of their downward pointing pistils. There are roses, bright pink, still early in their buds, and I know there will be more: yellow, and then white. At the back side of the fence, the clematis vines bring promise, and the raspberry bushes start with their white buds that will soon be fruit, along with the grape vines, trumpet vines, snaking around, sturdier than the furniture surrounding. There are forget-me-nots, dotted all throughout, delicate as the bandages I remember of my childhood. Like the lily-of-the-valley: petite, but abundant in their presence—as if a tiny army, telling me they got me. The lilacs start to fade, and the beauty bush in front is starting to turn pink again. The hollyhock leaves are full and wide, and I imagine the buds I'll find tomorrow or the next day. There will be more lilies. The ferns are tall and green. Wild geraniums. Spanish bluebells. The giant alliums: tall with purple balls like spikes. Solomon's seal reminds me of taller versions of the lily-of-the-valley. I have townships of them surrounded by big stones. I go to the garden store, per my ritual more than once every spring. I buy annuals that I'll hang from hooks I'll stake into the ground in the front yard and the back. White and red and pink and blue and orange and every color I can find.

Pipette

She sleeps a lot. Her therapist claims it is her engine. She understands science, having worked years in the lab with spectrophotometers and machines that spin and whirl. They give out numbers, producing results, and when the quality controls are off, the whole batch needs to be repeated. When she worked in the COVID lab, the machine never seemed to work right. She'd pipette. She cleaned the machines. She wore a mask, lab coat, gloves. She wanted to like it more. There were people all around, attached to their agendas. She liked the humming of the machines, the smell of petri dishes, the routine of putting set reagents into their compartments. Even after all her experience, with one machine the controls hardly ever came out right, and the next shift would have to do it over. This machine took a long time. There were all kinds of false positives, probably negative ones too. The shift lasted until midnight. She'd drive home to her dogs. They leave her without filters. These days, she's on sabbatical and in her dreams, she continues to pipette. There's no need for controls. Everything turns out right.

Breaking Bread

My dad sits in a greenhouse, glowing in the dark. He says, Pass the peas.

I see his brain light up like crosswalks I hardly saw in childhood, having grown up on a farm, though I imagine the crosswalks of his brain, all the different voices, and I wonder, if his voices have a color, would they be bright and neon? Or like death, the fall? Pastel, maybe gentle? Do the voices shout or whisper? Do they laugh like he sometimes did out of the blue, as if he had a secret? Or do they yell the way he yelled at me when I was just a girl and cried because I had a headache or a cough or was scared and felt I had to vomit? Do his voices make him scared? After he died, when I went to clean out his apartment, a medical card was in his wallet saying he was paranoid. A schizophrenic.

I knew something was wrong, but I never knew his diagnosis. My mom left him when I was young, and after that my dad's parents said I was a sinner. They put me on a ride and left me spindling. They said to be ashamed. They said they had no doubt. Later, as I grew into an adult, I tried to reach my dad. My grandparents wouldn't let me, and then they died, leaving me with nothing.

My dad couldn't hold a conversation. He was at a halfway house and when I tried to visit, sometimes he shut the door, sometimes he stood there, staring at me, crying. His eyes looked absent, sometimes mad. Sometimes I feared that he would break me.

Now he wears sweatpants in the color of his farm clothes. Gray and forest green. A shade between the two, and he wears a pearl necklace, an heirloom I have in my jewelry box that was gifted to me when my aunt died. There's a tattoo of an ax on his forehead. He spins his chair, leaning himself backwards. He says, The loquats here are square and dull. He says, Up here, the snow shines and it makes the sky melt.

    He burps. He farts. He laughs and hands me a bread loaf and says, Say hi to god. He says, I dare you to break it. I dare you to eat it. I dare you to feel.

Botanical

I pick up the remains, sign away and put the box up front, giving it a seat belt, going miles across the country, home to my apartment. I talk to the box, asking are you tired? Are you getting hungry? Do you want to stretch your legs some? And I picture the ashes, poof, a cloud around them. Someone had found him in the hallway. He lived alone, and mostly stayed in his apartment, except when workers took him to the bank and to get groceries. They said it was their job; he was easy and pleasant enough. He wasn't always pleasant when I called, but I guess it wasn't his fault. When I get the box home, I don't know where to put it. Space is an issue. I put him on the desk by where I'd put his typewriter, along with the lamp that used to be his mother's. The next day, when I put my shoe on, I feel something gushy. I take off my shoe and find a grape there. I can't remember the last time I had grapes in my apartment. It happens again the next day, and the next day, in those same old shoes. I check the fridge, look under the bed, the desk, the sofa, and I don't find grapes anywhere. I start storing my shoes upside down, then away in Baggies. After a while I throw them away, and by a pair of new ones, but that doesn't solve things either. I don't have many shoes. I'm particular about my feet. I put the new shoes up on a shelf and look over at the ash box. It's perfectly square, the size of a jewelry box I had once. I open the box and look in. Nothing but ashes. I say to the ash, Hey Dad, and I wonder where he is now. I got a report from his last psychiatric visit, the hearing of the voices. I sit on the floor with the box and shut it. My father was a farmer. He wasn't a fruit person. I like grapes, though they're not my favorite. I pour a glass of wine and start to draw on the box. I start with a stem, but that's as far as I get.

Stay Awake

A truck hits my side of the car, ruining the panels. I was daydreaming of a boy I like, wondering what he's up to. I'm still bruised from the week before after a driver hit me on my ten-speed and I ended up in an ambulance. I needed tests and it was urgent, but not urgent enough to not wait for my mother. I lay there on the gurney, looking up at the white, just hoping for my mom; this is before cell phones. When the hospital called home, my sister answered. She called the nightclubs, looking for our mom. It's sometimes hard to find her. The medics cut my clothes off. One side of my head felt heavy. I went home and was supposed to stay awake because of the concussion.

This time my sister's the driver. She's one year older. My head hurts. I'm shaking and tell my sister I have to leave. I can walk home. It isn't far. She says she's OK. She says she's fine. She keeps saying it over and over.

The Closest Thing

She gives me her hips. Mine do their sway and we know how to be sexy. Her hair is red and mine is blonde, the fake kind. We dance like we're equal, partly for my boyfriend. He's a bouncer.

We got matching tattoos the night before. We figure it was dumb, but we're allowed to be dumb once. Here, my boyfriend isn't really a boyfriend, though he's the closest thing. She's indifferent about him. I've slept with him enough to know he's at least OK. There's the music, and oh, up here: my friend. I love her like my sister. We tell each other secrets. She pulls me in. I look down at my boyfriend. He seems to admire us.

My Inheritance

As the daffodils in my yard begin to fade, new flowers come forth. Tulips. Solomon's Seal. Lilacs. Before all of these were snowdrops.

It's only my second spring in my new home.

I have to take down a diseased sugar maple. It leaves a big scar in the front of my yard. I plant a Rose of Sharon.

The original owners were horticulturalists; this is my inheritance. There are lilies, ferns, roses.

I do my best to nurture them. I do my best to get rid of the weeds.

All Over the Planets

She imagines a gentler approach to life, herself as a petunia, somersaulting out of her skin. She watches real-life mysteries, people's lives ending in doom. Will people, in time, see her as an eggplant? In a tomato or a plum? She sees her aunt and grandmother. They take her flying all over planets she's never seen. She flies so high. She never sees her schizophrenic father, but they say he's out there. She dreams about dogs running away and coming back. They're still there when she wakes. Barking. They run down the stairs and beg to go out again.

Dramatic

My dog kills squirrels. She's a poodle. It's in her nature. My dad used to kill squirrels and bunnies with his rifle, and we'd have to eat them. I wasn't sure why. We lived on a dairy farm and were never short on food. I'm vegan now. Sometimes when I let my dog out, she'll return to the door with a squirrel in her mouth. Sometimes she runs around the yard with it like that. I used to leave the back door open, and she'd bring the squirrels in, sometimes half alive. I used to feel sorry for the squirrels. My dog makes everything seem so dramatic.

Delightful

for Ross Gay

Sitting at the stoplight, I watch the clouds move, wishing I was somewhere out in nature: the park, the woods, the childhood farm where I grew up, where I used to lay on my back on the grass with my sister and look up, naming clouds, in all their shapes and sizes. It's a cold day, wet, and I imagine my backyard, the soppy leaves that mob my lawn, the work I need to do to make it less sloppy. My neighbor's raked his leaves, the piles resting by the curb; and the neighbor next to him has raked his too. As the light turns green, I move my Honda forward, heading to doggie daycare to pick up my dog Venus. My shoulder is a switchboard. I turn right, my muscles twitching ever since my swim earlier this morning. On the speakers, I hear a book about delights, and I try to be delightful, thinking of swimming with my friend, her thanking me for coming to her mother's funeral. I had to cross the border; the drive was two hours each direction. I had a book of more delights to hear. I was delighted to see my friend's son who lives in Hawaii, her daughter who lives in the Carolinas, her brother, who lives in Nova Scotia. I was delighted to have met them all last year at her daughter's wedding. I'm delighted to hear the speaker of the book talk about the delights of his coffee, folks remembering his name, the delight of giving every student in his classes a big fat A, and he can since he has tenure. I think: how delightful! Maybe I'll give all my students As. I wonder if they'd come to class, if they'd blow me off, if they'd give evaluations. The speaker calls assignments invitations. How delightful, I think, as I turn into the lot. The doggie daycare is delightful: every time I enter the workers are so friendly, saying hello, telling me how lovely it is to have some time with Venus. When the worker brings out

Venus, Venus jumps on me gently, giving me her kisses. Hello there, V, I say, sure to pet her, taking time to rub behind her ears so she knows that she's delightful.

High and Wide

My aunt got my boyfriend and me a room at a place called the Tundra: themed with deer heads, buffalo, tigers. It had a water park. My aunt left beer in the fridge, wine sitting by the hot tub, chocolates, bread and cheeses. She said she was glad we were late, since she couldn't get early check-in—it was the best room in the county, and the hotel bragged to host a princess, with autographed pictures hanging in the lobby. The room was high and wide and over woods on a private campus. It was snowing. My aunt wore a Packers jacket, a wool hat with earmuffs. She focused on my boyfriend. My boyfriend had an accent. My aunt tilted her head and listened as my boyfriend talked about his newest composition. A dance. My boyfriend thanked my aunt for the cabin, and I corrected his English. I asked my aunt if she could stay, but she said she'd call the next day to find out what our plans were. But we didn't have plans. After she left, I complained to my boyfriend, though I don't remember what for. My boyfriend said we should enjoy ourselves, since we'd taken off from work and the drive was so horrible.

Billiards

The poet said to all the listeners: I've always wanted to meet her. He read his love poems, dedicating them to her, calling her sweet vegetable names like rosy radish and artichoke candy. He said he read her work. People listened. He read a fuck-me poem, every line starting with a Fuck-me.

The students and teachers and the poet went for drinks afterwards. The poet leaned over to her. She was a teacher and bought him a drink: the best and straightest whiskey. The place was a dive, and she drank 7-Up.

He smoked chimney-style, ran a hand over his head, raving about supper.

They played pool. Her boyfriend was somewhere else. A student brought her a beer and she said thanks and went up to the poet. He said he wanted to kiss her, hitting a stripe, knocking in a solid. She stayed there, close, grabbing his cue for a shot.

On One Side

She remembered him calling from the bridge in San Francisco, hotels in Tokyo and Moscow; she'd be on one side of the country, and they'd meet in places with balloons and dynamite, so into their affection, they rose out of their engagements with bruises. Now they were apart again, and he wrote to her, saying he was desperate.

That wasn't how they'd started all those years before: as if she was in control, letting him think he was doing the controlling. No, she said. There was no way. She was nice at first. She'd write him, saying hi. Hello, she'd say.

But that wasn't how it went. She put on her shoes and ran forward.

Her Way

The ex called and said he wanted to explain. She was curious and thought about the fields they used to pass as he drove them to the park to walk along the pansies. He said, "I thought of what you said. About the last time." He said, "I want to explain." He said, "I went to high school with her. Before that, I'd never slept with any woman from my country." As he proceeded, she remembered his last visit to his country, how she called and he kept putting her off. They'd broken up months ago. "*Now* you're telling me?" she said. He said, "I would've lost you." She laughed and she said he lost her way before that.

Rare

She ordered beer and talked about gutting. Fish, the dew in her hair, the valley. After twenty years I found her. She said she always dreamt, but there were icicles from childhood, swords. She talked about the man she thought had been my father. We ordered steak, and the waiter asked how well and of the quality. Life. Her lips were big and her eyes were wide.

About the Hour

The closet wasn't all bad. She moved the shoes over to get comfortable, and there were her mother's boxes, and she wondered what it was like to be a catfish in water, a saguaro cactus, a tomb. She didn't know the time, but figured it was about the hour of English, where her teacher would be talking Rilke, maybe, and she almost wished she was there now because she kind of liked her teacher, but it was too late to come out, after hearing the sound of her mother's heels heading out, and then the garage door, and then the voice of her mother's cousin, who owned the house where they lived. And then the cousin's boyfriend, who she knew more about than anyone. She could tell from what she heard that he was in now. She was tired and didn't have the energy for much. She heard his footsteps. They kept getting closer and she leaned. She pressed her weight, feeling the resistance. She made herself strong, holding the door shut.

Spoonful

On our second date, we met on the upper level, where we dirty danced under flashing neon. We ate Mexican food and he said he should probably check his glucose, but maybe he'd be OK, and he sipped more, and later, I was only able to wake him with a spoonful of honey. He finally came to, asking where we were. Nights later we talked about mythology and geometry, the shape of objects, and I took off my clothes and looked in the mirror, then turned around to find him passed out on the bed again.

Please, Just Come to the Door

He tried to climb up. Him, on a rope, though I'm not sure how it got there. My sister and I had rented a hotel room. It was just any hotel, with leftover perfume, drapes that hung like cardboard. Not the cedar of our childhood, that chest our mother always kept locked at the end of the bed. I didn't remember him trying to come to the door. Our father was never like that. My sister and I weren't talking. Not that we were upset with each other. We just never really had much to talk about. We could sit in silence for hours, just looking at each other. It was something we'd just had to eventually get used to. I was probably thinking of a boyfriend, of the one I was probably in love with. I was probably wishing I could call him. I was probably wishing he'd be available in some capacity other than his capacity. Those were the guys I went to. My sister's husband liked to tell jokes when things got serious. I wasn't sure where he was. I really wished he was there. I wanted a good joke then. Maybe I was sipping. Beer or wine or vodka. I was usually drinking more or possibly quitting.

First, I saw my sister. Then heard something from the window. I looked down, and there was again our father. My sister came back from somewhere with hammers. She said it was the best she could do. We hammered that rope. Our dad was like a dragon. He got closer. A hammer does nothing when you're trying to cut. I asked my sister if she thought a knife could be possible. Our father kept on getting closer. He was climbing with more effort. My memory was fucked. He was crying. His head was bald. I could see it, looking down on the top of him. After a while he got closer. I kicked him down.

For a while, my sister and I sat there. We didn't really say much. She got a glass of water and said she had to go to her husband. I said OK, wondering about cops, if we'd have to file a report, but they never seemed too concerned before when we'd tried to report him. My sister and I waved, she left, I went back to the sill. It was dark, with stars, and a few city lights.

Existence

The home has turned into a workshop for creative writers. There's no air conditioning, but the writers don't seem to mind, wiping the sweat from their brows, as if it adds another prompt, something more for them to write about. I investigate the jewelry box of my grandpa, seeing his rings, thinking I might want one. I'm not so intrigued with the creative writing class. I'm more intrigued with the jewelry. I'm not sure why it's still here. Everyone knows my grandparents are dead, the house no longer in existence, but I want something to hold on to. From my grandpa's box, one ring looks nice. My grandpa always gave me special attention. I'm not sure why I don't deserve to have a ring of his. The meds don't always work, says someone from the workshop. I fly out of the room. One of the writers, on a speaker, asks where I am.

Life-Sized

My uncle's gained weight since I last saw him. His hair's gone gray. He says to forget about his birthday. He laughs a little, says, I don't have birthdays anymore. We're in someone's attic, where rodents scurry, and a life-sized dancer made of chocolate moves to the tunes of music boxes of my childhood. The dancer is limp and loose, not something you'd expect from a dancer made of candy. The tune is "Dance of the Sugar Plum." One I used to play on my piano. After dancing for a while, the dancer removes her candy skin and becomes an actual person. She sits at a desk and asks who my mom is. I look to my uncle, fat and round. He has new hair on his chin. His ears seem to have grown larger. I ask him, Is this what happens when you die? The rest of the family comes to join: my sister, my mom, and some of her cousins. My uncle doesn't really know them. He's my uncle on my dad's side. The candy dancer walks around with a ruler, pointing to us, focusing it back to me. I'm not sure if she knows what happened with my uncle, our bond, the ways that he would touch me. It wasn't always like that. It happened when the two of us were grieving after my aunt died. My uncle tells me he doesn't quite belong. Why, I ask him. Stay. Before he flies off, he promises he'll be back maybe another day for lunch.

Independence

It was the third of July, which meant tomorrow was a celebration: every year parades and fireworks, hot dog stands and corn roasts, the same vendors setting up balloons and water races. Ring tosses, prizes of stuffed monkeys, rock band T-shirts, mirrors with images of skulls, unicorns and horses. The penny toss, where you could attempt to toss coins into any bowl of fish and win that fish in a plastic bag. Tugs of war between legions, and a firemen's game, where teams of men donned suits, getting on opposing sides, aiming hoses up at an empty beer keg hanging from a clothesline higher than the treetops, trying to make their goal, everyone getting wet. Hamburger stands, where my Grandma and Grandpa Krupp worked for the American Legion, serving one-dollar cups of Pabst, my grandma wobbling from the hungry to the cash box, putting burgers on buns, my grandpa holding up the stub to show his missing middle finger, his smile getting wider, his wink tighter with every beer he drank. All this came after the parade, which started around noon, a buffet of 4-H and business floats, the shiny antique cars with their loud horns, the firetrucks shooting off their sirens, the bands marching, trumpeting off-key, and the American Legion with the old men aiming up their rifles, sounding on command. Clowns, people riding horses sideways, and the Old Old Ollie always had an exhibition on the back of his Ford, a skit of chubby shirtless men getting drunk on brandy.

Beforehand, the parade lined up at the high school lot, waiting for the town's noon horn, the sheriff leading the pack. The whole town was on vacation. Sidewalks, lawns filled up with folding chairs and blankets, strollers and umbrellas. The town was usually quiet from the outside. Now people sat and waited with their beverages and fans, radios, repellent, babies, bottles, bundles. Kids carried empty paper bags that would house their future Tootsie Rolls and Dum-Dums, treats tossed from the parade. Some ran onto the street, grabbing handfuls. As a child, I watched, never brave enough to leave the sidewalk, content at collecting what landed at my feet. My sister Shelly was the same way. We were shy, preferring the safety of our bedrooms.

One Fourth of July my aunt had a baby, and while news went around, my mom and her siblings celebrating at the beer tent, I sat on a swing, thinking about babies, getting sprinkled from the firemen's game, watching people as they shot darts and tried to pop balloons then hanging onto stuffed dogs and unicorns and wieners—I watched the little fish getting hit with pennies, people carrying them away in plastic baggies. My mom never let me play those games, saying it only wasted money. I wanted to try so badly. I thought maybe I could win. The park was always packed, people moving from the lawns and sidewalks after the parade, some indulging in an afternoon of baseball, some lounging at the beer tent, some playing games or watching them, some just sitting on the grass, nurturing their children. Fireworks were like any other fireworks. I was afraid of them.

At home, we had three channels, a TV with a round knob, where we'd watch shows like *Fantasy Island* and *The Love Boat*, my dad having a thing for *The Dukes of Hazzard*. It was the only time I saw him laughing, watching Boss Hog in his white suit, smoking his cigar and saying things sarcastic. We'd be sitting on the brown sectional, on one of its square pieces, and I'd be more interested in my father's laughing than the show itself, thinking what did it take for me to make him laugh? There were many nights of eating Cheese Puffs, all of us on our parts of the sofa, in the living room, watching that same show, with Daisy Duke and her long legs, heels and shorts, and then I'd watch Bo and Luke trying to outsmart, speeding up and around and away and over things in their fast red car.

I was thirteen. After a 4-H card party, where my father won the door prize of a pound of cheddar, he went around the farm on his John Deere beeping its horn, waving to my mom and Shelly and me. He didn't eat at dinnertime, and I was used to him devouring. He sat there stirring up his mashed potatoes with a spoon, tried cutting with a knife, dotting the arrangement with the peas and corn from my mother's garden. None of this was normal, and my mom said she was trying to get him to pray harder, that he needed church. I said OK and went about my business, listening to the radio, finding the top forty. My mother mowed the lawn, Shelly was quiet in her bedroom and I painted my nails in the bathroom—sitting on the toilet, lid down, my foot up against the roll holder, putting paint on my big toenail, feeling kind of pretty, thinking of Jeff, a boy I liked since kindergarten: blond and blue-eyed, always smiling like a secret. We had lots of secrets, the two of us saying in our notes things like, "You're cute." And "I think I really like you." I was admiring my toes when I heard my dad yelling, "Shelly, Elle! Come out!" I met Shelly in the hallway. We went out. Our dad told our mother to stop the mower. "Stop!" he said, holding his hand up like a policeman. He said, "That wedding's for us!" and I figured he was talking about the reception that he and my mom planned on going to that night after church. He hugged my mom, then stepped back and said to Shelly and me, "I love you! I love you all!" He laughed and cried and spun around and then he even hugged us. He walked away. My mother re-started the mower. Shelly went to her room. I went back to the bathroom, looking at my figure, my face, lining my eyes, trying on different shades of make-up. While my father finished milking, my mom and sister and I prettied ourselves in our respective places.

We went to church, like usual, my dad driving, my mother humming on the way, Shelly and I in back, looking out our windows. We parked, got out, all of us single file up the aisle, sitting in our usual spot, that same pew with a little chip on its end. I sat next to my father, Shelly on my other side, my mother next to Shelly. Next to my mom was my first-grade teacher, Mrs. Miller, who I always was afraid of, in her horn-rimmed glasses, her stiff walk and I heard of the horrid way she treated children, and although I never saw anything firsthand, just the possibility sent my mind in rages. I sat and prayed for the usual: for God to help the needy, for forgiveness, then thanking God for everything. Amen. I looked up, everything familiar, the same wooden pews, the same blue hymnals, the same organ playing in the background. I couldn't help but notice my dad's head down, like really down, almost between his legs and his hands were tight fists resting on his knees. He never got into anything except when he was yelling at home. At church, he was like a dead guy. He never sang, he hardly ever spoke. He didn't pray the way we were taught we were supposed to. Sometimes he fell asleep during sermons, and after he'd start snoring, my mother would tell one of us to nudge him. I noticed a bald spot on the back of his head, the hair on his neck, thinking he needed a haircut. Then he raised his head and shifted. He took those fists and hit them on his knees. He wasn't so loud at first. And he kept on banging: fist to knees, fists to knees. He was wearing brown pants. I glanced around. Shelly looked ahead and so did my mother. I figured probably nothing surprised them. I looked at Mrs. Miller. She stared at my dad nonstop, through her glasses. I nudged Shelly. She kind of motioned for me to look ahead. Mrs. Miller kept on staring, then her husband even, and then my father whispered loudly to my mother, "Help." I reached over and touched my mother's arm, poking her with a finger. Her skin was warm. She looked over and smiled at my father as if she didn't even know him, and then she looked at the altar, and then the pastor came out. I saw him step up to his pulpit. I looked up with everyone else and he started with announcements. I listened to the beginning of something, and then my father yelled, "God help me!" He said it a few times, then faded out. I shifted closer to my sister. My mother finally got up. She made her way around Shelly and me, and then she took my father, pulling him up and away. I watched them leave, and didn't know what to do, so I just stayed there. I wondered if Shelly might have some answers, but she looked blank. I moved closer to the aisle. The pastor moved on with his announcements. He told us all to sit and he invited us to pray.

Smiley

My neighbor's dog is lost. I've had a lost dog once, or maybe even twice, and three or four times. Growing up on a farm, my family had outside dogs. They weren't allowed in the house. The only leashes my family owned were the ones attached to halters to show cows and heifers at the fair. Our dogs were never fixed. They'd run away while in heat and come back (if they came back) gifting us with puppies. They were mutts. Back then there wasn't doggy DNA, but if there was, my parents would probably never go through the trouble. My neighbor's dog is a lab mix. Layla. She's friends with one of my dogs. They often play either in my yard or in Layla's. I have three dogs: Crunch, Smiley Face, and Sneeze. Crunch is a goldendoodle, two. Layla's two. They often exchange kisses through the fence. Over the fence. Under it. Smiley Face and Sneeze are rescues: smaller, older. I've had them DNA tested. Sneeze is a Japanese Chin. Smiley Face is Miniature Doberman Pinscher, Chinese Shar-Pai, Papillion, Husky, and some other things. Crunch has a high-pitched bark that goes off when she sees other dogs walking by with their owners. When Layla's out, they have their chorus. Layla's bark is more direct, perhaps more of a flat note. Crunch's bark is sharp, treble. Smiley Face and Sneeze hardly bark at all.

I see so many posts on social media of lost dogs. My dogs are microchipped, and on their collars are their names, address, my phone number. I have very tall fences, making it impossible for them to run away, but if they somehow do, my people can find me. I wonder where Layla is. If someone is gifting her watermelon, her licking from their fingers. If she's doing zoomies in a sunflower field under an eclipse. If she's waking someone's monster. Smelling turpentine, if she's planning on returning. I prepare an homage to all the lost dogs. As a child, I still remember Polly, run over by a tractor, my parents warning me not to view her body. She was a small dog. She looked like Smiley Face. I'd never seen a dead dog before that.

High as Streetlights

As the snow removal efforts continue, workers find more bodies. A looter's been caught on tape stealing a bubble gum machine. There are already forty lives lost. There's footage of the thief on tape. There are records of a four-month-old dying in the cold, a man about to be a father, nurses. The blizzard came so quick and there are snowbanks that rise as high as streetlights. The snow will melt and then it will cause flooding. I imagine people finding a random arm, a leg, clues to what's underneath. There are John and Jane Does in the morgue, and still on air, our authorities are fighting. One apologizes for things said. The other claims he's hardly slept. I decide to take a bath and pretend to be an experimental bubble gum machine. Maybe I'm a red one, or a blue one or a white one. Maybe I'm the bubble. Maybe I'm the shoot that sends the gums out.

Sleepwalker

At the ballet, I imagine the dancers jumping out into the crowd. The crowd seems to me a bit pretentious. I'm here for my birthday. Me, a farm girl, never going to ballets nor operas as a child. We had little performances, where I once played Mrs. Mott, a sleepwalker, and once a mouse. As a sleepwalker, I stepped with eyes half closed and arms out, in a checkered bathrobe. I almost fell off the stage. As a mouse, a mouse behind me stepped on my tail, which exposed my underwear. After the ballet, I go to my room at the Y. The man in the next room continues to be the man in the next room: his voice like large paws that fall into my dreams of donuts with my sister, our father continuing to saw down the hemlock trees in the yard and the hemlocks kept succeeding and growing on without him. My dad is dead. The opera lives on. The ballet! The man's voice in the next room doesn't stop. I finally knock on his door. I ask him to stop. He's a big man. Me, I'm very little in size, but I'm very large otherwise.

Go to the Clouds

On the plane, I think of horse and buggy days and wonder if folks ever imagined what it was like to fly. I look out to the layer of clouds like fuzzy carpet, the orange sunset like a sheet above it. I make a mental note, as I usually go to the clouds in my imagination when my hypnotherapist guides me. I tell myself to get busy feeling good and centered. Traveling screws up my sense of feeling grounded, but then I think I'm in the air after all, far from where gravity usually pulls me, and I think it's odd that I go to the clouds to find my center. I take a sip of water from my bottle that I bought for a fortune at the airport. Still not as much as the one that I ended up taking from the fridge in my hotel room. I should have just drunk water from the faucet. It was a good fifteen dollars and I'm usually thirsty after a long day of walking. The woman next to me sips whiskey and says, "When in Nashville, I drink whiskey. Smooth as butter." I say, "I can't drink the brown stuff. Clear stuff either. Unless you're talking water." She says, "My young guy screwed me over. Stole my taco business right down to the salsa. Damn shoestring of a penis. Write things down or else." I think of the last guy I was with, the sacrifices I first thought I was OK with. The plane jolts and my ear pops.

Confetti

She isn't usually an early bird and wonders why today she's awake by six a.m. She feels rested enough and the dogs have already asked to be let out, so she opens the back door, makes herself some coffee with the Keurig, then does her usual routine of opening the curtains, blinds, letting her imaginary fairies do their things every morning: helping her rise, their wings like little windmills. Her hypnotherapist tells her she's a deva and that's what got her into fairies; she figures it's not a bad thing for a fifty-year-old to think of while living alone. She has three dogs. Her daughter is grown and doing her own thing in the Peace Corps.

She's an ultra-marathoner, competing in trail races. Her next one is coming up and every day in training (and while not in training), she thinks of her body climbing, her legs in motion, her heart rate rising, her body struggling then her brain telling her she's strong. You got this, her brain says. Her body complies. Her brain and body remind her "self" there will be a race, and even if the race gets canceled, she still has to train, because it likely won't get canceled. Her brain tells her soul, her body, that it's worth it. Today's supposed to be her rest day. She puts a curtain over her face, one resembling the veil from her late mother's wedding. It's not a horrible thing. It isn't pleasant either. She imagines all the dumb confetti. She imagines herself a nugget into the possibilities of what her life might have become: her mom still around, if her father wouldn't have dropped her off to live with a man he said was his best friend. Her dad didn't have a best friend. She became a servant. She isn't sure where her dad is anymore. Isn't sure about the man. She moved away and put herself through college, had her daughter. Raised her. Today her toe hurts. It throbs. She goes to the freezer and looks for an ice pack.

The Man

The man jumped from a high-rise. The news doesn't say how far. The news says he was 52. The picture shows his bright blue eyes, his smile. The news says he has a wife and children. The news says it was suicide-awareness week. The news says that he was an executive director of a counseling program in charge of suicide awareness. The news says he was in his new position for six months. The news says that before that he was at another position at Cornell for over ten years. He gave Ted Talks on the subject. Before that, he was at the University of Southern Mississippi. That's where I met him. I'm not sure why I first started counseling there. I wasn't eating much. I was down to a hundred pounds. I'm a creative writer and was writing about a lot of stuff that I hadn't been able to write about before: my dad's schizophrenia, my mother's codependence, my own complicity in it all. The man gave me a three by five card and wrote on it: "I'm not responsible for anyone else's feelings," and for a long time I carried it around, studied it. The man had a nice smile. A good sense of humor. I once saw him eat an orange. His office was filled with books and I'm not sure if his office was comforting because of the things in it or if it was because I liked him. I'd told him about my childhood sweetheart who had killed himself with his own handgun in his twenties and seeing his gravesite unexpectedly on the plot next to my grandma. I told him a lot of things, and each time I left his office, there was always another person maybe like me perhaps waiting to tell him of another problem. Once or twice as I waited, he couldn't see me because he was dealing with another crisis. My issues were chronic, not acute. My issues felt important. He read my books. We'd kept in touch. His face was a wonderland.

Around the World

As a toddler, my son, when I was in the Air Force, would find blankets and safety pins, and we'd make capes for him. He'd swirl around rooms, pretending to be Superman. We lived around the world: England, Germany, Mississippi, Illinois, Wisconsin, North Dakota. I left his dad after the Gulf War when my son was just a toddler. His dad was my husband, then. My husband then was sent overseas during the war. He came back a different person. My son and I lived in places where one wears sandals, places needing firewood, places where maple trees are prevalent, places where people believe in gnomes, places where I started to believe in them myself. My son was always with me. After the Air Force, I worked in hospitals. At one hospital, during snowstorms, when I was on call, the cops would pick me up to take me to the hospital, and since I was a single mom, I'd bring my son with me. Nights, he'd be wrapped up in a blanket, bundled in the backseat of the cop car, and while I was doing my testing, he'd do his best to try to go back to sleep in the breakroom. I didn't get called in unless there was an emergency. Because the hospital was so small, I had more roles than just the testing. I'd have to go to the ER, collect blood from arteries, veins, and chaperone if a patient needed chaperoning. Lots of people died there. Lots of people came there bloody and had to get helicoptered elsewhere. Those days in the lab, while my son slept, or at least tried, I'd revive the lab doing my tests, hearing the machines click and whoosh and whirl. On occasion, my son, still in his pajamas, would enter, saying, "When can we go home, Mom?" These days, when I ask him about it, he says he can't remember. He doesn't remember much of our hard times. He remembers seeing ghosts in the yard. That's not something I recall. He's in the army now. Infantry. He's going to Ukraine.

I wish him a safe trip. He's still on my phone plan. He tells me he is fine. I tell him I am fine. I like to think we all are fine now.

Underwater

It's another day in the pool, and my swimsuit starts feeling like a custom-made tuxedo. Underground, with no neckline, made of fins. This becomes my make-up. I see the markings of the pool under the water as I swim and envision weeds. I'm constantly in water. When I reach the ledge, I'm reminded I am human. I catch my breath, talk to other humans, who like me, do their best to become the best versions of themselves as they can without being under.

Into the Nose

She peels oranges, slices carrots, puts them, along with the spinach into the nose of her big juicer. It's a bear of a machine, growling, spitting out liquid into the bowl, the pulp oozing out yet another spout. She adds a bout of ginger, its shape like a toe, then feeds the juicer cherry tomatoes that may only have a day left. She asks them, why are you so fat? Pushing them in, her internal thermometer so hungry. She craves nutrients, sunlight, dusting off the weathered air of snow, wind, hanging onto the winter like too-low hanging earrings. Her mom always told her, as a child, if she wore big earrings, her earlobes would sag down to her shoulders. She was glad when she grew older for the knowledge of a half-truth.

Snout

Lula finds another shoe. She takes everything she finds—or tries to steal—into the sunroom. It's a newer shoe, one without her teeth marks. Girl, I say. I offer the teddy bear I bought for her the day I brought her home. Its tummy squeaks if you press it. I take the shoe back. Little girl, I say. I'll make you a confession. She tilts her head. I say, I thought you would be easy. My two smaller older dogs, Will and Fay lay in the living room. Fay snores, Will looks in my direction; his only two teeth jet out under his lip. When I brought Lula home from the Airbnb where I met her—I was there for something else—she wasn't ready to come home yet—I had to go back to get her. She was eight pounds then. Now she's over fifty. I don't eat meat, but I cook it for my dogs, along with rice and veggies. The lights go out. I step into the kitchen, feeling around on the table for my flashlight. In the distance, I hear sirens. The dogs perk. They bark. They sit, raising their snouts.

Studies of the Senses

When he plays his piano, his chords ring softly in the sunlight. His dog barks at who might be coming to the door. Later on, he records his music in his studio, that was once, before he owned it, a child's bedroom, balloons wallpapered on the walls, and then, there were cries and coos ringing all throughout that baby's bedroom. Now he strums his old acoustic, and this woman, who stands outside, waiting by the door, she only wants to listen. She hears him playing, and the wind is a slight whisper. The dog is no longer barking, and this man has ceased playing his guitar and singing, from what she hears, so she puts her finger to the doorbell, and she remembers that this ringing is defective, so she knocks lightly on the wooden door, underneath its window, and she hears him say, "Come in," as she's often heard before. She hears the dog approaching, hearing the eagerness throughout his panting. After she arrives, you can hear them softly talking. If you are outside, you can't hear what they are saying. Maybe he is offering her a beer, or maybe he is telling her about an encounter with a stranger. If you are inside, you can hear him recalling events of his day, how he got up and practiced early in the morning, how his hands ached because he'd been pressing on his ivory keys throughout the noon and evening, how his fingers bled from strumming his guitar. He might ask her how her day was, and it might take her a while to answer, because mostly, she just tries to listen. She really only wants to listen. Sometimes they are laughing. And sometimes, you can hear the movie that is playing on his laptop. This is after all the talking. There is silence, mostly. There will be the movie playing, and they can hear the dialogue together, curled in his bedroom, under the warmth of his sheets and down, and they are so close, they can hear each other breathing.

Sometimes, when they on sitting on the porch, they can see the stars. One time, when she was coming over, she saw his shadow through the window. He was playing his piano, and she watched his long and slender arms. She found it elegant, eccentric. She only wanted to stand outside and watch the beauty of their movement. She closed her eyes, and wondered what he might be playing. She loved to imagine, for she'd heard him play before. But now, she was only seeing. She loved what her eyes said about what she'd heard before, what they left for her sound imagination. She knocked on the wooden door, underneath the window. She sensed, and saw him coming to the window, and she remembered then that it was him, as if, since yesterday, she had forgotten. He was tall and slim, and today he was wearing a white T-shirt, plaid shorts, and a pair of Nike sneakers. His wire glasses sat snugly on his nose, and she knew, by the glowing look of him, that he was working really hard, probably looking at his notes, his fingers synchronizing with the keys of his piano, and she saw something in him that she always wished she'd had, a talent for beautiful, extraordinary music. She saw him smiling down at her, and then, again, she saw him, leaning in to her. He was offering her a kiss, so she closed her eyes, and she let her intuition lead her. There wasn't darkness as she kissed him. Then she opened her eyes, seeing the man smiling, and she was smiling back at him, and then she looked down and saw the dog, big and black, and wagging, so accepting, as if she would never be a stranger, and she leaned over petting him, and she felt as if she belonged, as if she were a member of their household. She looked away for just an instant, and she saw a lot of things, like his stereo, his grand piano, sheets of music that were piled like a platform. She looked back at him, and she wondered how he saw her.

He once told her, that, with her, he doesn't want anything romantic. He said he doesn't feel it. He said he didn't believe it. She remembers when he told her. She doesn't remember when it started. She heard nothing else. She always wanted to ignore it.

Steam rises from his kettle. His house smells like aftershave. And it smells like French Roast, or maybe cappuccino. It's a humid scent. It isn't quite the summer, although the weather teases us, telling us it could be. The man doesn't smell anything right now, not that he can notice. He is practicing his music. He is playing his guitar, writing a new song, although he doesn't have the words, isn't thinking about lyrics. Right now, chords and notes and scores are all that matter. He might smell the burning of the kettle, after it is empty, and the burner gives off an eerie scent, but he won't notice right away, and when he does, it is not the scent that first alarms him. When the woman arrives, she notices the remainder of the burning scent. She also notices the familiar scent, the one that always lingers, not knowing why it might remind her of some other place or time or maybe some ex-boyfriend. She doesn't know which one. Maybe it is bleach, or wood polish, or maybe window cleaner. She smells him when he leans over, into her, when he offers his embrace. She accepts it. She loves his naked scent. She knows that he's been working because she notices a hint of sweat that reminds her of when they are together, sleeping, and she loves this part of him, this part that maybe only she, and none of his other lovers, might remember. She smells the dog as he comes between her and the man, separating them, as if he is their only toddler, begging for all of their attention. The dog smells like any other dog she can remember. She never really liked the scent of dogs, but now, there is something endearing in this scent, as if this is a small detail of this drawing, this picture of this home, this place, this life of this man who is her friend, who is blessed with gifts and intuition, this man who is her lover. She leans down, petting the dog behind his ears, and his body moves like a flimsy stick, and she smells his breath, and she breaths into him. "Pretty dog," she wants to say, but we are talking about smells here. Sometimes other things are more essential.

When she remembers what he said, about not wanting anything romantic, she is disappointed. Yet she is, maybe, unknowingly, relieved. This could mean that she will not be threatened, not be afraid that they will get too close, but this also means that he will be looking for another. He tells her that she is not the one. She does not believe that anyone has a one and only. Maybe she will never have to tell him all there is to know about her.

This night, when she arrives, she sees a reflection of him sitting, his arms outstretched, and she thinks, by what she is seeing, that he is inside, playing his piano. She wonders what he might be playing. As she is getting closer, she sees that he is outside, sitting on his swing, and the lights from the inside are glowing out at him, thus, showing his reflection. As she approaches, she sees that he is smoking. She sees the movement of his arm, his pointed elbow, and she imagines that he is inhaling. She sees the end, and yes, he is inhaling, the light is faintly glowing, getting brighter as it is expanding. It is burning. She sees the swing, then she is sitting next to him, and she is with him, swinging. They are looking at a tree. The tree is planted in the front, and in reality, it is all that they are seeing. He says, "That tree looks like a hand," and she looks at it, at the trunk, and she sees that the trunk is like a wrist, and the branches are all fingers. She puts up her hand, looking at her fingers, that once played on her piano, looking at those fingers in all of their extensions. "Yes," she says. She believes that he is right. She is in agreement. She says that it looks like the state where she is from. She reminds him that she is from Wisconsin. She loves seeing all these things. There is beauty, hope. It gives her something to believe in.

This night, when she is in his bed, she wakes up crying. She cannot stop herself from crying. She can barely hear herself. She hears him ask her what is wrong. But she doesn't know. She says she doesn't have an answer. Later on, after she is quiet, she hears him breathing in his sleep. She hears him, saying the next morning, telling her, that after the crying, she was talking in her sleep. She was speaking, shouting, reciting something, calling out in repetition. She hears him tell her she was almost singing, like she was talking to a devil, to a god, or maybe to somebody's ghost or to an angel. He says she was chanting. She says she doesn't know how she could do that. He says he's never heard anyone sing or speak that way before.

Sometimes, they go out for coffee. The texture of those wooden tables, they are smooth, and some of them are rough, depending on the perception of your fingers.

At the coffee shop, he tells her that he loves her. He is working on his laptop, and she has come to visit him between the teaching of her classes. She hears this man, telling her he loves her. But there are so many other things around, the clanging of the glasses, the people talking, ordering a drink or maybe two, a bagel, or a salad. Some of them around the other tables are conversing, whispering small, or maybe some important talk with one another. Chairs behind her are being pushed aside, and she hears them as they rub against the hardwood floor. She watches his green eyes. He is wearing a green shirt. It is her favorite. It glorifies the color of his eyes. She is ignoring everything around her.

This woman has no other lover. This woman has a roommate, and a cat, and a job teaching disadvantaged children. She once had a child herself. She once had a husband. But this is not that story. This is not the story of her husband or her child. This is a story about seeing, smelling, hearing. This not a story about what this woman has forgotten, not a story about childhood. This is a story of this woman's need, of her indulgence. It is not about her brother or her father, or about a man who might have raped her. This is a story about senses. This is a woman who has wanted. This is not about what might have happened with her husband.

They go to the movies. They smell, they eat the popcorn. They see previews, the actors, the credits on the screen. They hear the people talking. They feel the salt of the popcorn on their fingers.

He believes in something. What he believes in she will never be a part of. She wants to believe in something beautiful and lasting. She listens to her senses. She is hearing, smelling, seeing. She is watchful, being.

The birds wake them in the morning. They squawk outside the bedroom window. The dog comes into the room, and barks along. They have not set the clock. She says she has to go. He looks at her and asks her to come over later on and listen to his music. She does not remind herself that she will never be the person who he dreams of. She already knows this. She is listening. She will go to work, and she will teach the children. She reminds him that she loves him. She wants to hear his music. He smiles. She says she will be back. She knows that he is watching as she's leaving.

Sketches of Her

Sleep in as long as you like, the mother says to her newborn, who is stubborn, sucking, pawing day and night. She dreams of sketches of her childhood. She cradled dolls, changed fake diapers. She invented bedtimes. She was spanked a lot. She had to take her clothes off. She felt her father's belts. She understood the sting. After each time she'd stay alone in her upstairs room and remove her dolls' outfits and say, "What did you do wrong?" The dolls looked at her blankly. She'd spank them, rock them, spank, until it was time for her to go down again.

Cellar

My mom was afraid of thunderstorms, so we'd hunker in the cellar. On the piano, she'd play the "Elephant Waltz" and my sister and I would dance in our pajamas. We'd sip on pretend teacups, though upstairs we never had tea. Downstairs housed freezers filled with meat from the cows we butchered, ones we'd raised. There were things like tongue and tail. I remember the animals as calves. I'd weaned them from their mothers. Mixed their formulas and fed them. The cellar was always dusty. The floor was dirt, and cold. There were mice droppings. There was a staircase leading to a door that went outside, though we never used that door. From outside, I saw it leading in. The stairs to the first floor of the house had a handrail. The first floor was the kitchen, the living room, a bathroom. The second floor had bedrooms. My dad lived there all his life, and as far as I knew, his dad too, and, from what I heard, the dad before him. The road shared my last name. It was named after my family. My dad was in the barn a lot. We had a big farm. My mom was in the kitchen a lot, cooking. My sister and I could always kind of sense when our dad was nearby. My mom tried to please him, him always walking around with his hands shaking. He never really said much, but when he finally did, it was loud and shouting. Summers, when he was out in the field, our mom would turn on the TV, to the channel where women her age wore fancy diamonds, somersaulting around in clothes she said she was too fat for. She'd make us stuff like grilled cheese and tomato soup, which was a treat for us, because she said she was busy preparing the next meal for our father. There were times when I was sick, and I couldn't stop myself from coughing. At night in bed, I'd hear my father from the next room yelling for me to shut up. I tried my best to conceal my coughs. I wasn't sure then where our mom was. My sister would help me by putting a pillow over my head. There was nothing else we could do to stop the cough. I'd tell her to try harder. She did her best. We were successful at some things. We got straight As in school and became experts at pretending.

Machinery

Speak to me, I say to my dog. He barks, an hallelujah. I make kale chips, blending cashews in the blender with olive oil and garlic. I knead the greens. As I quiet my device, the Spanish music from the next room voices a crescendo. I used to make baby food in the blender, juice in the juicer, saving the pulp for muffins. I have dug out these appliances from boxes, though I moved here two years ago with my boyfriend, into this little kitchen with only one outlet that's powerful enough for my machinery. I say to my dog, No news, please. His head cocks. It cocks again. On the radio, the president talks of war. I served in a war in the Air Force. I was a medic. I collected blood. My son's in the army, serving in the tropics. There are pictures of him with ammunition strung across his body like a necklace, a sash. My son, he shaves his head. There are videos of him and his soldiers in their night gear, vision goggles that make everything look green. I can hear their breaths, the sounds of their boots. He lifts weights. I picture him at night with his wife, his dog, his one-eyed kitten. I picture myself with him, so tiny, after his emergency delivery because he was losing oxygen.

Marathoner

Sometimes the door tries to close, like a heat wave in a dance class that even snow won't cure. Years after the bombings, it's as if the door's still open. Nothing can change hearing one noise, then another. The sea of people rushing down the street. I was alone. I'm a runner and was never fast enough to qualify. I'd taken pictures at a corner near the finish, then got hungry and stopped at a cafe. At first, I thought the noise was thunder. The skies were clear. There were sirens. Lines of police, firemen, people coming in and out, crying, asking about loved ones. An official came into the cafe and said we had to leave. We were herded down the street. I went back to my hotel I already had checked out of. I couldn't get to the airport. No planes were leaving. My phone didn't have a signal. Speakers told us calls on phones could maybe set off more bombs. The hotel went on lockdown. People hung out at the bar. The place ran out of food. People didn't have rooms anymore and ended up sleeping in the lobby. In the morning, there were guards and SWAT teams. They wouldn't let us out of the hotel without a valid ID. I wandered. It was like a movie, though I was alive.

Runaways

Hurry in, I say to the dogs in the car, and we move fast as runaways. Outside, the wind howls, and I think of the phlox about to bud, and with the rain, my mind goes to my flippers in the pool, the bulkhead that keeps moving, confusing triathletes like me who try to get our yards right when reporting to our coaches. I imagine the snowdrops flowering outside, looking like teardrops on a pillow: thousands and thousands of them, and I want to touch them all and tell them their presence is a dream. At the pool, I think of things like nightstands of my childhood, taking naps, dreaming of the smell of my mother's cupcakes.

At home, my three dogs move their legs, all of their twelve paws making imprints on the floor. They eat the food I free feed. They drink from their shared bowl. I look at the marks they make. I take them outside to the back garden, and we get wet in the storm. The wind blows. We do the best we can to stay upright.

Jumper

I was a high jumper in high school. I loved running towards the bar, twisting my body just so, headfirst, angling my back. My tailbone surfing, then landing on the cushion. I was a sprinter my first year, winning the one hundred. I was also a long jumper, and then the triple jump. Building my speed, giving my body the momentum to carry me ahead. The velocity, in the high jump, up. After that, I ran cross country. I played basketball, a guard, feeling wicked as a tiger. I had the agility to move quickly on my feet and steal from my opponent. In softball, I played pitcher, sometimes shortstop. I loved being in the center of the mound, taking aim. It was underhand, and my arm was fast. In volleyball, I was one of the short ones, but I had a good serve. I was good at setting. Diving, feeling protected with my kneepads, elbow pads, and I loved being part of a team, doing our rotations. One year I was a cheerleader for the wrestlers. I'd sit on my pillow with my sweater and short skirt, moving pom-poms: roll-em over, lay em flat, pin the shoulders to the mat. I took swimming lessons as a kid. I rode my bike along the country roads, and when I got older, into town with my friend, where we'd find places and boys we could make out with.

On the farm where I grew up, there were early days of feeding calves, and then cows. Summers of baling hay and picking stones. My sister and I would race each other to the barn. We'd practice our gymnastics, hanging from the clothesline. Before the words of schizophrenia, divorce, how a set of grandparents can decide to disown small and loving children because their dad is ill and they move in with their mother. Before that, I spent most of my time with animals: the cows, the goats, the farm dogs that never really lasted, getting run over by a tractor or running off because they were in heat. I tamed the wild cats when I could, bringing them pieces of cheese that I stole from the fridge and hid in my pockets.

I love planes and the smell of their fuel. It reminds me of the Air Force, the many miles I used to run along the flightlines, where I recalled my life as a jumper, building my momentum. I imagined rising so high that I'd morph into a plane, taking myself into the clouds and far beyond, hanging out with all kinds of angels for as long as I wanted.

Candy-Striper

I've been reading too many books, I tell myself, lately. People polluting other people's minds. Candy-stripers licking off the salt of a random person's parts. Cellular towers losing power, making everyone go mad. I go to a meeting on campus. I've been on leave for a long time and I could have opted to stay at home, but there are things to address. There are colleagues, with various agendas, sitting at a table. There are things we don't agree on. There's an air quality alert. Fires spilling over from Canada. Even though it's another country, I'm so close I can see it and wave to it every day if I want.

Hybrid

She imagines divorce committees all over the world, asking themselves: What's for breakfast? It doesn't seem a bad life: hers. Perpetually single. Especially compared to all the segments and true stories that keep showing up on *Dateline*. What could be worse? It's finally spring and before even checking emails, she finds forget-me-nots with open eyes all over the yard, as if they've had sleepovers with the daffodils and tulips, saying, we've been dormant for so long and where the hell were you? Her email in-box is chubby, mostly spam. Even before coffee, it's easy to filter out the same old. She goes through the lala of her morning, like a harmony, imagining a person in a top hat. Before she heads to the station for a small escape, she dons high heels, a dress. She brings her dog. A hybrid. She tells him he's notable.

Climbers

At home, in a trinity of voices, my dogs howl and they whistle. One wants to go out, the other wants attention, and the other one's head is in a cone, healing from his stitches. Outside the moon wanes. One of the dogs, according to the vet, seems to have been attacked by a raccoon. I imagine a theater in my vet's mind, a raccoon? In my yard? I suppose one that's maybe rabid could find its way. My yard has a high fence. I've heard raccoons are climbers. Even with the cone on, my injured dog makes gestures. He has so many stitches on his face, his neck, his body, shaved. He has tear stains that make marks on the part of his face that's unshaven. He's thirty pounds: Chinese Shar-Pei, Papillon, Miniature Doberman Pinscher, Husky, other stuff. I feed him ice cubes. He can't bend down enough to eat out of his dog dish. The other dogs have been accommodating, friendly. I go into the sunroom, where I have buckets. Treats. I have three fractured ribs from tripping over the dogs last week. Climbing stairs. Good dogs, I say. I work hard to breathe. They sit for me so kindly.

Theoretician

I take an oath every morning when I wake to be better to myself, to maybe change, but then after letting the dogs back in, I go back to sleep, to the dreams where my dead ancestors still try to take over my domain. They try to rule my dreams, their projections on my veganism shame me by making me a child again and forcing me to eat certain things like pork chops. But my dreams make me a theoretician, and I can rise and be a fairy in my splendor. Even in my dreams, I can accept them, love them, or I can rise above, or I tell them to go to hell because I'm finally allowed to do, when awake, whatever the f I want.

Perennial

I start to think it's a crime for me to sleep in for so long. I sleep so hard, with dreams of old sweethearts, paper airplanes, and peach trees made of origami. I wear eye masks and ear plugs. Even after my dogs wake me, I fall back asleep and sink harder back into my dream world. These days, especially this season, I spend a lot of time there. It's winter, and I imagine the perennials outside, how they wait. How much energy does it take for them to sprout again?

Floating on an Ocean

I wake feeling dull but trying to remind myself there are miracles everywhere. Maybe a baby being born. Maybe someone found a feather. Maybe someone's floating on an ocean far away from here in a way that is transforming. I open the blinds, my usual lull. Dogs barking, asking to go out. I have a fenced-in yard. When I lived with my last boyfriend, I had to make him meals, had to hear him watching Fox, his talk about Trump. When I moved into my house, I listened to a lot of Taylor Swift. I blasted her on speakers. It takes some time to get used to freedom. And then come the chores. I have a whole lot of leaves in my yard.

Red Zero

I meet my friend in a thunderstorm. She's asked me to be her health proxy. I've just done up my legal stuff myself: will, proxy, power of attorney. Because one day you can be having pancakes at brunch, and the next thing, your loved ones are having to figure out probates, awkward people coming together to decide what the almost-deceased wants, or worse off, the deceased. It's a gift to not leave my loved ones in a stir fry on the table, hopping one-legged, question-faced like I had to do after my dad died. My friend says she doesn't hope to be in any situation soon to need a proxy. She needs to be sure her girls are taken care of. We order lemon martinis. We're the only ones in the restaurant, it seems. I drove through the rain, thinking of proxies. My high school English teacher died the day before. She was 92. She was also my mom's teacher. I was scared of her. I don't remember anything she taught me except her rule about bringing in half sheets of paper, and if there was a quiz and someone like me forgot, it meant a red zero, and four of them meant failure.

A Borrowed Canoe

I try to keep things moving. My bruised ribs, making me feel like a borrowed canoe. I can't lay on my stomach. I imagine myself as a custard-colored kite, rising above the sunrise. I try to swim and can't seem to get my breath right. I get cold in the pool. I shiver in the steam room. I ache and ache, and then later at home, when I try to eat my lunch, my tooth crumbles. I land in a chair at my dentist's office: yet another charge that I'll add to my debt. It's how these things go. Everything is one thing relieving the pain of the other. I've spent hours in the ER. It's just a bruise, but every time I breathe, it feels worse than the stab wound I got once in a brawl when I was the only survivor.

Plumbing

She's on her hands and knees, cleaning the toilet, which she calls super bowl. She gets around to the back of it, the front, the tiles, the walls. Next to it is the plunger she used to use more than once. She imagines the veins of the plumbing: the person who lived here before her and the ones before who had the house built. She bought new toilets after moving in. Fancy taller toilets, which her mom advised her were better once you get older and it helps if you have back problems. She's an athlete and the only back problems she's had are from training. She's fit. She can lift herself from the toilet. But she appeased her mom. Her mom doesn't live in the same state and has never been to her house.

It took her a while to adjust to the higher seats, and she sees the appeal. She remembers telling her mom, OK. She said, Let's make it safe again. She's happy with the toilets. She's mostly glad that she doesn't have to spend a lot of time there.

Neverland

I'm wandering in shallow water, people in costumes passing: clowns and superheroes, scarecrows. Athletes in wetsuits swim, wearing crocodile swim caps. Help, I say, but the words can't come out, and everyone ignores me. I cannot seem to wake. I see a bright blue sky, castles, a landscape like I've never seen, and I try to remember how I got here. Yes, I was teaching and fell asleep after giving students a writing prompt, then my soul flew out the window. I feel like a pheasant more inclined to run, yet my wings are useless. I feel the rush of water on my legs, treading through, pushing myself harder, then just like that, I'm back in the classroom, telling my students how dreams make such good fodder. Try falling asleep on a full stomach. I tell them my dream of not being able to wake from the dream, and I describe the dystopian world I was just a part of. The students' faces aren't familiar, and one of them has an adult-sized toddler. The other uses his long orange hair as dental floss, another smears lipstick on her forehead, her cheeks, throwing up balls that never land. I tell my students, Write down your dreams, please, but don't ever tell your reader it's a dream because isn't fiction dream-like? Don't ever end your piece by making your protagonist wake from a dream.

Speed Dial

I speed dial my way through yet another novel, hearing it on audio on the way to the dog park. There are two other lab mixes and a husky. I'm bundled up, feeling husky myself, with snow pants over my jeans, snow boots, two sweatshirts, a parka, gloves, a hat. On my bone-conduction ear buds, the story continues: a dystopian world, where people speed dial each other, ride motorcycles, delivering pizzas, and try to clear their yards with ice picks. It really doesn't feel too dystopian to me. I used a shovel earlier to break the ice on my walkway, my front steps. I used my tools to dislodge a loose bolt that was holding up my garage door. It would squeak and rumble, and then the thing would freeze. No way I could get my car out. I dislodged the bolt with a hammer, feeling like I won at least at something.

At the park, the puppy plays and wrestles. The humans with the husky say they are both Joe: one younger, one perhaps a grandpa. I turn off my headphones. One of the Joe's arms is in a splint, aiming it out past him at an angle. I say, That was me once. He was in a motorcycle accident. It's just one of a series of things he still needs to fix. I recall my hospital-working days; motorcycle accidents usually didn't end well. I throw the ball to my puppy for a while. Back in the car, I give my dog a treat, plug the novel back into my Audio Android, hearing more about dystopia. It feels so far away. Yet close. I'm eager to get back to my actual life, yet isn't this what I'm doing? I drive home. I don't want this book to end.

Acknowledgments

Versions of poems from *Contact With the Wild* have been published in the following journals: *The Big Other, Centaur, Center, Conjunctions, Denver Quarterly, Flash Boulevard, Five Points, Ghost Parachute, Lit Mag, Lit Magazine, Matter Press, Midway, Miracle Monocle, The Nation, Noo, NOON, Northwest Review, Post Road, River Teeth, SoFloPoJo, StoryQuarterly,* and *Willow Springs*.

About the Author

KIM CHINQUEE grew up on a dairy farm in Wisconsin and served as a medical lab technologist in the Air Force. She received a B.A. from the University of Wisconsin, an MA from The University of Southern Mississippi, and an MFA from the University of Illinois, Urbana-Champaign. She's the author of eight books, most recently *Pipette* (Ravenna Press, 2022). Her work has been published in hundreds of journals and anthologies including *Noon, Conjunctions, StoryQuarterly, Indiana Review, Ploughshares, The Nation, Dreaming Awake: New Contemporary Prose Poetry from the United States, Australia, and the United Kingdom, Buffalo Noir,* and others. She's received three Pushcart Prizes, a Henfield Prize, serves as editor of *New World Writing Quarterly,* associate editor of *Midwest Review* and chief editor of *ELJ (Elm Leaves Journal)*. She directs the writing major at SUNY-Buffalo State University, is a competitive triathlete, and lives with her three dogs in Tonawanda, New York.

www.ingramcontent.com/pod-product-compliance
Lightning Source LLC
Chambersburg PA
CBHW020335170426
43200CB00006B/398

Praise for Kim Chinquee

"There is a simplicity to her prose, much of it is pared back and precise. It takes some skill to write so sparingly and requires a self-confidence born from experience and commitment to the craft of writing. Chinquee is a clever writer who is always in control of her material."
—*IndieReader*

"Chinquee's measured prose breaks over the reader like shallow, slow-moving waves."
—*Kirkus Reviews*

"This is an author who knows how to take nothing for granted!"
—Kyle McCord, author of *Reunion of the Good Weather Suicide Cult*

"To read Kim Chinquee's work is to be startled, touched and affected."
—Pia Z. Ehrhardt, author of *Famous Fathers* and *Now We are Sixty*

"Kim Chinquee has the dead-eye aim and the precision with language that makes her stories hit the mark again and again."
—Jean Thompson, National Book Award finalist author of *Who Do You Love*